A Henmead Enterprises, Inc. Book
Edited by Harry M. Rubin.

Library of Congress Control Number: 2010901865

First published by AuthorHouse in 2010

AuthorHouse™
1663 Liberty Drive
Bloomington, IN 47403
www.authorhouse.com
Phone: 1-800-839-8640

ISBN: 978-1-4490-8131-7

Printed in the United States of America

CRÉER C'EST VIVRE™

The Real Alice in Wonderland

A Role Model for the Ages

By

C. M. Rubin

With Gabriella Rose Rubin

"I can identify with the delight that Alice Liddell experienced as a child, being in the company of Charles Dodgson, providing both muse and audience for his fantastic stories. Her face and what I can infer about her spirit are captivating, and it's not hard to see how she might have launched works of art which went on to rock the world."

- Lizzy Rockwell

Illustration by Lizzie Rockwell

The Real Alice In Wonderland
is dedicated to all those who guide, influence, and
inspire the minds and souls of human beings.
~ C. M. Rubin

I dedicate this book to
the Real Alice in Wonderland in my life

_____

To the Real Alice in Wonderland in my life:
My daughter, Gabriella Rose Rubin
C.M. Rubin

To the Real Alice in Wonderland in my life:
My mother, C.M. Rubin
Gabriella Rose Rubin

"Would You Like A Little More Tea?"

I grew up hearing my grandmother's stories about Alice, the aunt of my great aunt Phil, but I really knew very little of her heritage or why her association with Lewis Carroll's story was even important or relevant. I remember one warm July afternoon going to a "mad tea party" and hearing all the Alice stories again at the home of Great Aunt Phil, who was the daughter of Lionel Liddell, Alice's youngest brother. There was plenty of tea but no clean cups. Plenty of spoons but no white sugar lumps. When Great Aunt Phil's ponies swallowed the jam tarts before we could savor ONE, well, things got considerably curiouser and curiouser.

Flash forward - thirty five years later my daughter announced at Alice's Tea Cup in New York City, "Let's tell them the story of Alice Liddell." *Alice's Adventures In Wonderland* had been selected for her school's Book Day and she remembered we had a connection to the Liddell family. She hoped that mother and daughter could present a workshop about the real Alice in Wonderland. A little label on my tea cup said, "Drink Me." Gulp! We knew something interesting was going to happen. Lights, camera, action, we followed Alice Liddell down, down, down the rabbit hole, never once considering how in the world we would get out again.

Alice's Adventures in Wonderland

"Curiosity often leads to trouble," but piecing together Alice Liddell's riveting life story has connected us with previously unknown relatives and countless new global friends associated with Alice's heritage, all of whom have generously contributed rich experiences to our lives and fascinating content to our story. Most of all we connected with Alice – Alice, who did not seek fame, but when the world thrust it upon her, did her duty and triumphed!

Alice Pleasance Liddell

"Just as Alice's journey down the long corridor led to a beautiful garden, the story leads every child to the beautiful world of his own imagination."

**Esther Browning
The Story Museum,
Oxford**

Discovering Wonderland

Alice's Family

Alice (named after a Princess) Liddell (with an L) was born on May 4th, 1852, the month and day on which Lewis Carroll's *Alice's Adventures In Wonderland* is set. When she forgets her surname in *Alice's Adventures In Wonderland*, Alice does manage to remember it "begins with an L."

Alice was the fourth child of Henry and Lorina Liddell. She had two older brothers, Harry and Arthur (the latter died of scarlett fever at age 3). Alice had an older sister, Lorina (the Lory in *Alice's Adventures In Wonderland*), and a younger sister, Edith (the Eaglet in *Alice's Adventures In Wonderland*), and the three sisters were always very close. Completing the Liddell family clan were five younger siblings: Rhoda (the Rose in *Through the Looking Glass*), Violet (the Violet in *Through the Looking Glass*), Albert Edward (died at 8 weeks), Frederick, and Lionel.

> *"What's your name child?"*
> *"My name is Alice, so please Your Majesty."*

Alice's Adventures In Wonderland

Alice Pleasance Liddell

"**W**ho are you?" asks the seemingly ill-mannered caterpillar in Alice's Adventures in Wonderland. Victorian England was extremely conscious of class. The origins of a person's ancestry were more important than at any other time in English history. Alice's lineage was impressive. Her grandfather, Henry George Liddell senior, was the younger brother of Sir Thomas Liddell of Ravensworth, who was made Baron Ravensworth in 1821 at the coronation of King George IV. The family's magnificent ancestral home, Ravensworth Castle, was acquired in 1607 during the reign of King James I of England. The family's history from this date forward is rich with riveting stories of Liddells who left their mark during the course of their lifetime. There were famous adventurers, statesmen, writers, philanthropists, soldiers, and industrialists. Once upon a time, Ravensworth Castle in the village of Lamesley, North Durham, was the pride of the county. Today it is in desperate need of renovation, and initiatives to raise monies to rebuild it continue.

"Would you tell me why are you are painting those roses?" asked Alice.

"You see Miss, this here ought to have been a red rose tree and we put a white one in by mistake and if the Queen was to find out we should all have our heads cut off..."

–Alice's Adventures in Wonderland

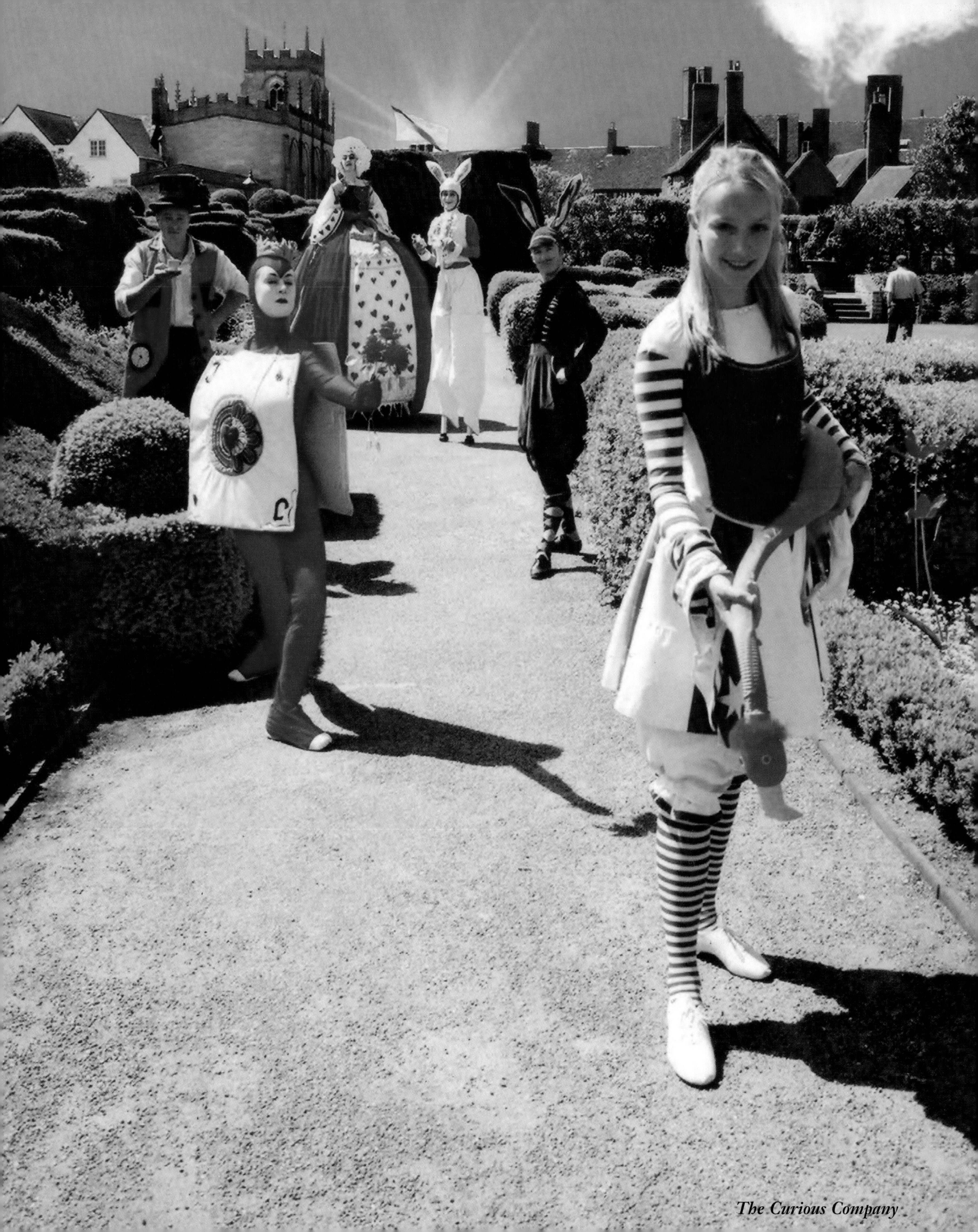

The Curious Company

Henry and Lorina Liddell moved their family to Oxford in 1856 when Henry was hired to be the Dean of Christ Church College, Oxford University. The London Times advertisement for Henry Liddell's job at that time as Dean of Christ Church announced: "The man we want must not only be a ripe scholar and apt to teach but a thorough gentleman, a man skilful and experienced in governing young men of the upper classes, a man of sound judgement, unflinching firmness, good temper, courteous manners, business habits and incorruptible integrity."

Dean Henry Liddell possessed all these qualities. His family motto was firmly upheld by both his appointment to one of the most powerful academic positions in England: Vice Chancellor of Oxford, and by the publication of his Greek-English Lexicon (nine years in the making), which he co-authored with Robert Scott. This big fat dictionary (used by Greek students today) had pride of place on the family bookshelf alongside the English dictionary. It was one of Oxford's and all of academia's definitive resource publications. Miss Alice Liddell was brought up in the ultimate house of words.

Fama Semper Vivit

Our Reputation Lives Forever

Liddell Family motto

HENRICO G. LIDDELL
DECANO
MDCCCLV — MDCCCXCI
ALVMNI DVO
IRM ET TVB

14

Dean Henry Liddell inspired the White Rabbit in *Alice's Adventures in Wonderland*. The Dean ate many of his meals in the Great Hall at Christ Church. Perhaps he was seen splendidly dressed, pocket watch in hand, scurrying along in a great hurry, exclaiming "OH DEAR! I SHALL BE LATE" (*Alice's Adventures in Wonderland*). The Dean even had his own little rabbit hole in the corner of the Dining Hall through which he was known to make his quick escapes.

"Oh! the Duchess, the Duchess! Oh! won't she be savage if I've kept her waiting!"
- Alice's Adventures in Wonderland

"It wasn't very civil of you to sit down without being invited." said the March Hare.
"I didn't know it was your table," said Alice; "it's been laid for a great many more than three."
— Alice's Adventures in Wonderland

16

In this period of England's history, Oxford University was the center of influence. The Liddells moved in the very highest social circles of their day because the upper echelons of the day sought their education there. Queen Victoria, The Prince of Wales, Prince Leopold, Sir John Stainer (distinguished British composer – The Crucifixion), Sir John Ruskin (eminent and influential Victorian artist), Sir Hubert Parry (distinguished British composer – Jerusalem), and other luminaries were visitors to the Liddell home.

Alice's father was respected as an innovative educator. He also had artistic talents. He made many architectural improvements to Christ Church college during his tenure as Dean. Lorina Hanna Liddell was a working partner in her husband's career. While he dealt with his many duties as Dean of Christ Church, she divided her time between their hectic social life, her parental duties, and caring for the College's male-only students, particularly when they got sick. As her daughters became older, Lorina's obsessive husband-hunting for them consumed a lot more of her time. Husband and wife were genuinely devoted to one another. Their secret to a long and successful marriage was that each dominated their separate spheres. Added to a genuine love for each other, they had important cultural interests. It is no coincidence that during the Liddell's time at Christ Church, the arts flourished.

I am the Dean and this is Mrs Liddell.
She plays the first and I the second fiddle.

—**Oxford rhyme about the Dean and Lorina Liddell**

An Oxford University Education

Alice inherited her father's significant academic and artistic talents. Further, she had the benefit of a superb academic environment. A large army of the finest Oxford tutors were hired to educate her and her siblings. They were overseen by the children's governess, Miss Prickett (also known as Pricks, who inspired the Queen of Hearts). Pricks was formal and strict, and took great care to ensure the girls applied themselves to their studies. Alice, who was a little more free-spirited (largely due to her never-ending curiosity about everything), believed Lorina was Pricks' favorite. Perhaps that infamous catch phrase, "Off with her head," was later created just to amuse Alice about the character of Pricks.

Pricks

Inside the Deanery (Alice's Home) today

The children were home schooled in the Deanery, as was the custom of the day. Alice enjoyed learning, but her best subjects were English literature, foreign languages (French, German and Italian), art, and music. In addition to academic studies, Alice and her siblings were expected to master the disciplines of fine table manners, etiquette, and general obedience.

Edith, Lorina, and Alice   Rosenbach Museum & Library, Philadelphia

"Reeling and writhing, of course, to begin with," the Mock Turtle replied; *"and then different branches of arithmetic - ambition, distraction, uglification and derision."*

Alice's Adventures in Wonderland

Inside the Deanery (Alice's Home) today

It was much pleasanter at home when one wasn't always growing larger and smaller and being ordered about by mice and rabbits.
Alice from Alice's Adventures in Wonderland.

Inside the Deanery (Alice's Home) today

Dinah's our cat and she's such a capital one for catching mice.

Alice from Alice's Adventures in Wonderland.

"Well there was Mystery," the mock turtle replied...Mystery ancient and modern, with Seaography...the Drawling-master was an old conger-eel, that used to come once a week: he taught us Drawling, Stretching and Fainting in Coils.

Alice Pleasance Liddell

Women were not admitted to membership in Oxford College until 1920, although they were allowed to attend lectures forty years prior to that date, and to sit examinations. If she had lived in a different period, it is very likely Alice would have pursued her higher education outside of the home. In 1886 (when Alice was in her thirties), Elizabeth Wordsworth, the great niece of the famous English poet, founded St. Hugh's College at Oxford. Despite conventional views on the role of women, Wordsworth was a supporter of improved educational opportunities, and her goal was to enable women to become financially and emotionally self-reliant. In 1986, the college turned co-ed, and today welcomes outstanding students from a great range of diverse backgrounds.

St. Hugh's College, Oxford

St. Hugh's College, Oxford

Alice of Llandudno

Dedicated to the memory of Geraint Wynne Morgan

Penmorfa

"I still have the happiest memories of Penmorfa and of the rambles over the Great Orme and among the sandhills..."

Letter to Mayor Of Llandudno, 1933, from Alice Pleasance Hargreaves

Dean Henry Liddell, his wife Lorina, five of their children, the footman, Mrs Liddell's personal maid, the children's nurse, Miss Pricks the governess, and an additional swiss nursery maid first began vacationing in Llandudno in 1861 when Alice was 9 years old. It was in this peaceful, scenic welsh town on the shores of the Conway Estuary and at the foot of the Great Orme Mountain, that Dean Liddell designed the family's large gothic-styled vacation home named Penmorfa. The home was built using glazed ruabon terracotta bricks (an expensive luxury at the time), and sat high above a cliff. Among the many famous guests who came to visit the family was the British Prime Minister, William Gladstone. Mr. Gladstone suffered from vertigo, and so the three sisters, Alice, Lorina and Edith, were known on occasion to assist the great politician down the steep path to the beach with his eyes shut.

Alice and Edith at Llandudno

A pleasant walk, a pleasant talk,
Along the briny beach.
– Through the Looking Glass

Penmorfa

Alice, the Dean, Rhoda, Edith, Lorina and a friend at the beach

Souvenir From

George Forrester, Artist

In 1933, the British Prime Minister, Rt. Honorable David Lloyd George, unveiled the famous "White Rabbit" memorial. Created by the renowned British mason, George Forrester, the statue was dedicated to Alice and Lewis Carroll.

GOGARTH ABBEY HOTEL

The sea was wet as wet could be,
The sands were dry as dry.
You could not see a cloud, because
No cloud was in the sky.
  – Through the Looking Glass

As the Alice books became more successful, so too did the fame of the book's inspiration, "Alice of Llandudno." An Alice trail and a Wonderland store became tourist attractions. Penmorfa was turned into a popular hotel. Alice stayed in touch with the town of Llandudno even after her family stopped vacationing there. The town is still proud of its connection to Alice today.

This is the famous white rabbit statue on Llandudno's west shore, created by the celebrated mason, George Forrester in 1930.

Charles Dodgson and Alice Liddell – A Unique Creative Collaboration

Edith, Lorina, Alice

Alice met Charles Dodgson, a Christ Church math professor and amateur photographer, at the college cathedral on April 25, 1856, when she was four. Mr. Dodgson (as Alice called him) was 24 years old at the time. He was photographing the magnificent church with his first camera, which he had purchased just one month before. In that very same month, Dodgson had also invented his pen name, "Lewis Carroll", for his writings, but it was nine years before *Alice's Adventures In Wonderland* would make that name immortal.

Dodgson, who dressed mostly in black, wore a top hat and always wore gloves, was a shy, awkward, upright man with a stammer. When Alice spoke about her memories of meeting him, later in life, she remembered thinking that Mr. Dodgson had swallowed a pole, since he always stood so stiffly. At that meeting, Mr. Dodgson photographed Alice's eldest brother, Harry. Upon seeing the photo, Dean Liddell, who was interested in the new art and technology of photography, invited Dodgson to become the official Liddell family photographer. It was his early work with the Liddell children that helped establish him as one of the significant photographers of that era.

Alice

Alice

Alice, Edith

Lorina

Alice

"Without Alice's infant patronage I might possibly never have written at all..."

Lewis Carroll writing about Alice Liddell

M r. Dodgson was happiest when he was entertaining children. It didn't take long for the Liddell children to connect with him, and since Alice's favorite expression was "Let's pretend", it didn't take long for Alice to become Dodgson's favorite child-friend.

She adored the fun escape he offered from the disciplined world of Victorian life at Oxford. The Liddells lived in the Deanery at Christ Church, directly across from Dodgson's home. It was here Dodgson would meet Alice, Lorina and Edith to play their favorite outdoor game: croquet. Mr. Dodgson created a special version of the game just for the girls, called "Castle Croquet". The children played under a famous tree where we imagine they might have seen a cat without a grin or even a grin without a cat.

The "Cheshire Cat" tree, is still in the Deanery garden today. A little door connects two gardens behind the Deanery. This door took a "little golden key" to unlock it, the inspiration for another tiny magical door in Alice's Adventures in Wonderland.

Alice

"I recall that he was the kindest of people to small children"

Alice Liddell speaking about Charles Dodgson to the New York Times in 1932

"*Get to your places!*" *shouted the Queen in a voice of thunder, and people began running about in all directions, tumbling against each other; however, they got settled down in a minute or two, and the game began.*

The Queen, from Alice's Adventures In Wonderland

Oxford Botanical Gardens

The awkward Don spent more and more of his free time with the Liddells. Mr. Dodgson took his "ideal child-friend" (as he referred to Alice) on fun outings to places like the Botanical Gardens and the Natural History Museum in Oxford town. Here, Alice could see the Dodo bird. The Dodo bird appears in *Alice's Adventures in Wonderland* and is still in the Museum today, along with a tribute to The Real Alice, i.e. Alice Liddell and her story.

Oxford Natural History Museum

Alice's Shop

was used by Lewis Carroll as the Old Sheep Shop In Through The Looking-Glass. Alice Liddell visited this place regularly as a child, to buy her barley-sugar sweets. It was a grocery shop run by a woman who sounded rather like an old sheep!

Mr. Dodgson would take them to buy barley sweets at a grocery shop run by an old lady with a bleating voice (inspired the story of the Old Sheep Shop in *Alice Through The Looking Glass*). The grocery shop was situated close to underground streams and was prone to flooding. The Oxford locals started calling it "Alice's Shop" after the Alice books became famous. Today, Alice's Shop is world famous and a treasure trove for Alice themed souvenirs and memorabilia.

The best treats were Mr. Dodgson's boating expeditions in and around the Oxford area. The most famous one of all time is the one credited with the creation of *Alice's Adventures In Wonderland*. This took place on Friday, July 4th, 1862.

Here is Alice's version:

"Mr. Dodgson told us many many stories before our famous trip up the river to Godstowe near Oxford…….He seemed to have an endless store of these fantastical tales, which he made up as he told them, busily drawing on a large sheet all the time. Sometimes they were new versions of old stories, sometimes they started on the old basis but grew into new tales owing to the frequent interruptions which opened up fresh and undreamed of possibilities.

My eldest sister was 'Prima'. I was 'Seconda' and 'Tertia' was my sister Edith. I believe the beginning of 'Alice' was told one summer afternoon when the sun was so burning that we landed in the meadows down the river, deserting the boat to take refuge in the only bit of shade to be found which was under a newly made haystack. Here from all three came the old petition of 'Tell us a Story,' and so began the ever delightful tale. Sometimes to tease us – and perhaps being really tired – Mr. Dodgson would stop suddenly and say, 'And that's all till next time.' 'Ah but it is next time,' would be the exclamation from all three; and after some persuasion the story would

start afresh. Another day, perhaps the story would begin in the boat and Mr. Dodgson, in the middle of telling a thrilling adventure, would pretend to go fast asleep to our great dismay."

–Alice's Recollections of Carrollian Days, 1932

It was soon after this trip that Alice began to urge Dodgson to write down his story.

All in a golden afternoon, full leisurely we glide, for both our oars, with little skill, by little arms are plied, while little hands make vain pretence our wanderings to guide.

Lewis Carroll, poem in
Alice's Adventures In Wonderland

Illustration by David Cooper

"Although Carroll sent his close friend Alice down the rabbit hole in his far fetched tale, he never left her uncared for. The characters, as strange as they were, all helped young Alice grow by becoming ridiculous obstacles that she overcame. The story is a great adventure made to empower the young Alice. To me it is a true gift of love."
—David Cooper

The only reason that Alice in Wonderland, among the countless stories Carroll told got written down at all was that she begged him to.

Stephanie Lovett Stoffel, Author,
Lewis Carroll in Wonderland,
Discovery News Interview April 19, 2001

"It does not do to think what pleasure might have been missed if his bright eyed favorite had not bothered him to put pen to paper. I started to pester him to write down the story for me, which I had never done before. It was due to my going on and on and importunity that, after saying he would think about it, he eventually gave the hesitating promise... which started him writing it down at all. The result was when he went away on vacation he took the little black book about it with him, writing the manuscript in his own peculiar script, and drawing the illustrations. Finally the book was finished and given to me."

–Alice's Recollections of Carrollian Days, 1932

On November 26, 1864, Lewis Carroll presented Alice with her book, *Alice's Adventures Underground* (the title Carroll chose after considering alternatives such as Alice's Golden House, Alice Among the Elves, Alice among the Goblins, and Alice's Doings in Wonderland). Carroll had spent over two years writing and illustrating the book for Alice. The manuscript consisted of ninety two pages covered with his print like writing as well as thirty seven of his own pen and ink drawings.

" When I examined the little manuscript...I, for once, agreed with the description in the auction catalogue. It was stated therein that it is 'hardly too much to describe this most attractive literary manuscript...It's general appearance, as well as the remarkable vigor and imagination of the author's drawings (many of which Sir John Tenniel followed very closely) is familiar through the facsimile published in 1886, but it does not convey more than a suggestion of the extraordinary delicacy of the penmanship and the intimate association of the drawings with the text. There is a charm inherent in the manuscript which defied transmission to the printed page'."

"A Christmas gift to a dear child in memory of a summer day."

Inscription in Alice's Book from Lewis Carroll

Dr. A.S.W. Rosenbach, speech in New York in 1932

Rosenbach Museum & Library, Philadelphia

Alice Liddell and Charles Dodgson — The Break Up

Illustration by Tatiana Ianovskaia

"I have not seen thy sunny face, nor heard thy silver laughter;
No thought of me shall find a place in thy young life's hereafter—
Enough that now thou wilt not fail to listen to my fairy-tale."

—Lewis Carroll, ***Through the Looking Glass***

Illustration by Tatiana Ianovskaia

A break up occurred between Dodgson and Alice's mother, Lorina, around the time Dodgson presented Alice with *Alice's Adventures Underground.* All outings on the river and on the Christ Church campus between Alice and Dodgson were forbidden. No one knows for certain why Alice's mother did this. Could Dodgson's beautiful gift have triggered the concern? One only has to look at the handcrafted exquisite work of art to feel its creator's deep connection to Alice. Did Lorina see it as an expression of Dodgson's deeper feelings for her child? Was he hoping to marry her daughter one day?

Alice was at the age Victorian parents started looking for suitable husbands for their daughters. Lorina was an ambitious and powerful woman with a controlling influence on Christ Church's social life. Dodgson was an undistinguished, poor professor whom Lorina would never have considered eligible.

Alice was leaving her childhood behind. She was becoming a woman; a beautiful, intelligent and cultured woman with a mother who had big ambitions for her. Around Alice's 12th birthday, Lorina forced her to destroy every letter she and Dodgson had exchanged over the years.

This experience was one of the great traumas in Alice's life. Being a respectful child, she had no alternative but to bow to her mother's wishes regarding the relationship. However, one can imagine how shattering, how deep a test of character this break up would have been. Lorina wanted to end a creative collaboration with one of her closest friends, her mentor. Alice not only had to tolerate this, but she had to find the inner confidence to recover from a tremendous loss.

Without Carroll's and Alice's collaboration, the world would never have experienced the greatest children's book of all time. Further, who knows going forward what other creative projects Alice might have inspired him to create.

"Unfortunately my mother tore up all the letters that Mr. Dodgson wrote to me when I was a small girl. It is an awful thought to contemplate what may have perished in the deanery waste-paper basket."

— Alice Liddell

Alice Liddell

"Who cares for you?" cried Alice. "You're nothing but a pack of cards!" At this, the whole pack rose up into the air, and came flying down upon her; she gave a little scream, half of fright, and half of anger, and tried to beat them off...

Alice's Adventures in Wonderland

"Oh I've had such a curious dream!" said Alice…and when she finished, her sister kissed her and said, "It was a curious dream, dear, certainly; but now run in and get your tea; it's getting late."

Alice's Adventures in Wonderland

Alice Liddell

The breach between Lorina Liddell and Lewis Carroll made it difficult for Alice and Carroll to meet up. Meanwhile, Carroll received an offer from Macmillan to publish the story while he was still working on the hand-written manuscript. Carroll, obsessed that Alice would get too old to enjoy his story, was determined to present her with both versions at the same time.

This was not to be. As the publishing process began, Carroll needed complete control over the creation of *Alice's Adventures in Wonderland*. Ultimately, he self-funded the production of the book to avoid interference from Macmillan. Hurt by her mother's attitude towards Carroll, Alice secretly stayed in touch through Miss Prickett on all matters related to its publication.

Dodgson hired John Tenniel, a well-known professional illustrator, to create the art. Dodgson wanted the real Alice's identity protected, and so he selected another child to be Tenniel's model. Alice had already developed a talent for art, and Dodgson wanted Tenniel's illustrations to be perfect for her. Understandably, Dodgson was not easy to please, and no surprise that Tenniel never illustrated another children's book after the Alice books.

John Tenniel Rosenbach Museum & Library, Philidelphia

Just in time for the third anniversary of the famous July 4 boating trip, two thousand copies of *Alice's Adventures in Wonderland* were printed with red vellum covers. A unique white vellum bound copy arrived special delivery for Miss Alice Liddell at the Deanery. Dodgson actually recalled this first sample due to a quality control problem. On December 14, 1865, Alice received her revised dark blue morocco vellum copy of the new first edition of *Alice's Adventures in Wonderland*.

It was just the beginning of Alice and Carroll's unique collaboration. The book that had brought them together would always keep them together.

We can never know exactly what special quality Charles Dodgson saw in the young Alice Liddell that moved him to create "Wonderland". I have painted several works inspired by the characters of Wonderland, but my favourite is "Queen Alice". I have portrayed her as a sort of Divine Child archetype - or maybe she is simply a child, like Alice Liddell, posing for Mr. Dodgson's camera, having raided the contents of the dress up box, to act the part of a Queen.

–Frances Broomfield

Queen Alice

©Frances Broomfield
Courtesy of Portal Gallery London
Photography i2i

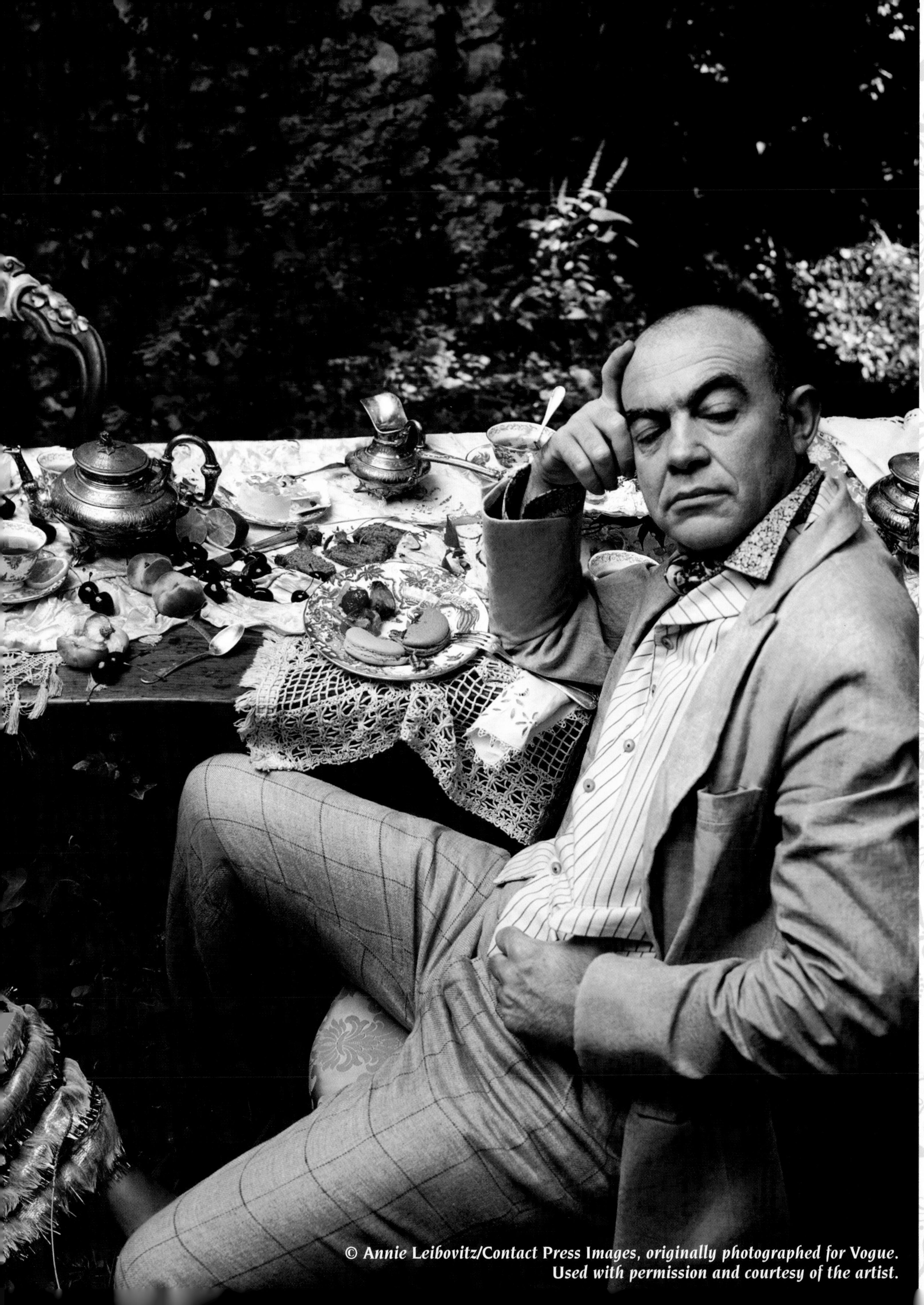

Alice Doll by Madame Alexander Dolls

Beyond Wonderland

Alice the Artist and Alice the Model

Many artists and photographers during the course of Alice's life were captivated by her beauty and her talent as an artist's model. Alice was also a gifted artist herself. Sir John Ruskin, one of the most eminent and influential Victorian artists of his day, knew her as a child and became her teacher when, as a young woman, she enrolled as a pupil in his art school. In 1870, she won the school's first prize for an artwork. Another one of Alice's artworks was framed for permanent exhibition in Ruskin's school. Alice enjoyed a special student/teacher relationship with the great man.

Ruskin

"I have sent you a little vignette of Turner's — which you must not be frightened by, as if it were too difficult . . . you will need no skill to copy his works."

Sir John Ruskin to Alice Liddell

Alice

Artwork by Alice Liddell

The Beggar Maid

Charles Dodgson was one of the foremost portrait photographers of the 19th century. His most famous photograph was his portrait of Alice Liddell as the Beggar Maid, probably inspired by a poem called The Beggar Maid, written by Alfred Tennyson in 1842. The photograph has a wonderful intensity about it, and clearly the model and the photographer had a special rapport.

"It's the gaze that holds us and makes the photo seem so unlike any other portrait of a child – it's the subtlety and complexity of Alice's expression, the paradoxical mixture of the sly and straightforward, the saucy and serious: the intense concentration that Alice brought to Dodgson's portrayals of her as a child."

Francine Prose in
The Lives of the Muses

Charles Dodgson

"Being photographed was a joy to us and not a penance as it was to other children. We looked forward to the happy hours in the mathematical tutor's rooms."

Alice's Recollections of Carrollian Days, 1932

After his rupture with Mrs. Liddell, Charles Dodgson photographed Alice professionally one last time. The so-called "Last Sitting" took place in June, 1870, when Alice was 18. Her mother accompanied her to the sitting.

The Sisters

In the summer of 1864, Alice, Lorina, and Edith posed for up to ten hours a day so that the distinguished artist, Sir William Blake Richmond, could create one of his most famous paintings. It is called "The Sisters". It was painted at the Liddell's country home in Llandudno against the background of the Great Orme, Llandudno's famous mountain.

Sir William Blake Richmond painted the portraits of the most eminent people of his day. Alice's daily contact with great artists, such as Richmond, increased her passion for drawing and painting. Richmond regarded this particular work as a milestone in his career. It was well received by the critics. All three Liddell sisters were very beautiful, but Sir William had this to say about Alice:

"Little Alice, to whose pretty face and lovely coloring no reproduction can do justice, is seen on the right in profile, peering at the big volume on her sister's lap."

William Richmond writing about Alice Liddell

In the 1870's, Alice's beauty inspired another distinguished photographer, Julia Margaret Cameron. Julia Cameron was known for her photographs of celebrities of the Victorian age. One of her most famous series of photographs is of Alice. This picture was taken at the home of the popular poet of the day, Alfred Tennyson. Alice is photographed against a romanticized background of flowers. It is said that Prince Leopold (Queen Victoria's youngest son) became entranced with Alice when he saw this picture of her.

Julia Margaret Cameron

The English poet Sir Henry Taylor had this to say of Cameron's photos of Alice:

"I have hardly seen any photographs of hers which are more beautiful in themselves or seem to represent more beauty in the person photographed…than her photographs of Miss Alice Liddell."

A boat beneath a sunny sky,
Lingering onward dreamily
In an evening of July–

Children three that nestle near,
Eager eye and willing ear,
Pleased a simple tale to hear–
Long has paled that sunny sky:
Echoes fade and memories die.
Autumn frosts have slain July.

Still she haunts me, phantomwise,
Alice moving under skies
Never seen by waking eyes.

Children yet, the tale to hear,
Eager eye and willing ear,
Lovingly shall nestle near.

In a Wonderland they lie,
Dreaming as the days go by,
Dreaming as the summers die:

Ever drifting down the stream–
Lingering in the golden gleam–
Life, what is it but a dream?

Poem by Lewis Carroll

The Men Who Loved Alice

The Pierpont Morgan Library & Museum, New York

"She was entrancing as one would have wished Alice to be."

Arthur Houghton Jr.
Interview, Publishers'
Weekly 1962

It was not unusual for men like Lewis Carroll (Charles Dodgson) to have close but platonic relationships with young children who were idealized and romanticized as Victorian emblems of purity and innocence. Alice Liddell was Carroll's "ideal child friend" and his role model for the character of Alice because she was kind, bright, creative, and tenacious. Alice knew Carroll adored her and she used this fact to get him to create *Alice's Adventures Underground* for her. He had entertained many other children with his fantastical tales, but none of them had ever inspired the awkward, shy professor to do something with them. Perhaps he thought the stories trivial or perhaps he lacked confidence in his fairy tale writing abilities.

Maybe he simply lacked motivation. Whatever the reason, when Alice Liddell pushed him to make a special effort for her, he delivered. *Alice's Adventures Underground* empowered its child heroine. From Alice's perspective, we believe she strongly connected with Carroll's theme, and that it inspired and motivated her to take command of her life.

As a child, Alice helped Carroll become a universally respected literary figure. It is reasonable to assume that he felt indebted and completely devoted to her, even more so as time went on and his fame increased. If he was in love with Alice, this love was unrequited. There is no sign of any inappropriate behavior between them. As further evidence, when Alice had her first child, she asked Carroll to be godfather, which in Victorian times would have reflected significant respect and trust.

"What wert thou, dream Alice, IN THY FOSTER-FATHER'S EYES? How shall he picture thee, Loving first, loving and gentle, loving as a dog and gentle as a fawn; then courteous to all, high or low, grand or grotesque, King or caterpillar, even as though she herself were a King's daughter, and her clothing of wrought gold; then trustful, ready to accept the wildest impossibilities with all the utter trust that only dreams know; and lastly curious – wildly wildly curious, with the eager enjoyment of Life that comes only in the happy hours of childhood..."

Lewis Carroll for Alice Liddell

As she grew into an even more beautiful, charming, and popular young woman, Alice inspired the devotion of other men. Disappointed suitors cherished her memory for years, even after they were married to other women.

Prince Leopold, Queen Victoria's youngest son, met Alice while he was an undergraduate at Oxford, and soon a romance blossomed. Leopold's and Alice's love of music, art, literature, and languages were natural bonds. The subject of matrimony was discussed, although to avoid any kind of scandal, it was kept secret by the Liddell family. Alice's mother thought Prince Leopold a great match for Alice, and the family gossiped that he wanted to marry her. The matter is mentioned in a letter kept by Alice. Unfortunately, Queen Victoria would not permit her royal son to marry anyone less than a Princess. The lovestruck couple ultimately decided their union was not destined to be. Alice's deep love of family and sense of duty were more important to her than her own personal happiness.

Prince Leopold

Throughout their lives, Leopold and Alice remained very close. When Alice did eventually marry, Leopold's beautiful wedding gift (a jewel encrusted horseshoe) was sewn onto the bodice of her wedding dress. After Alice's marriage, Leopold married a princess per Queen Victoria's wishes. Alice wrote to Leopold on the birth of her second child, asking Leopold to be Godfather to his namesake. Leopold replied:

"I shall have great pleasure in being so. Our child will probably be christened on Easter Monday, we mean to call her Alice."

Prince Leopold to Alice

Tragically Leopold died a year after his only child, Alice, was born. Alice was deeply saddened by his death, but the memory of their forbidden love lived on in the names of their children.

On a boating trip with the Prince, Alice accidentally gave him a black eye with her oar. Prince Leopold wondered "What will the Queen say?". Alice concluded "I was never beheaded."

Alice Liddell - recollections of Prince Leopold

I shall think of you tomorrow for you know how I have felt and sympathized with you...in your joys as in your sorrows.

Prince Leopold to Alice

Lord Winchelsea, the twelfth Earl of Winchelsea, was rumored to have sought Alice's hand in marriage. Shortly before his death in June, 1898, he wrote a touching farewell letter to Alice in which he expressed his lifelong love for her. He told Alice, "before this reaches you I shall be no more". He writes about the time spent with her and her family as "a time in one's life never to be forgotten," and bids her goodbye with the words "I hope you will have a long and happy life with all my heart…"

Reginald (Regi) Hargreaves

Reginald Gervis Hargreaves was an extremely wealthy country gentleman known to his friends as Regi. He was an undergraduate at Christ Church from 1872 to 1878. He first met and began courting Alice in 1875. Although he was no match for Alice academically, Regi was a charmer and an enthusiastic sportsman. He fell madly in love with her. To Regi, Alice was the epitome of good taste and the finest breeding. Unfortunately for Regi, many men were enchanted by Alice's talents, and for all her mother's efforts, Alice did not seem in a hurry to become engaged.

My Darling Alice,
Do you think of me as often as I do of you, I wonder. It will take up most of your time if you do.

Letter from Regi Hargreaves to Alice

Dear Alice,
I send you the last photograph that was taken of myself. With it I send my warmest and most heart-felt wishes....you know how I have felt and sympathised with you and yours in your joys and your sorrows...

Letter from Prince Leopold to Alice

Ave Dulcissma, Dilectissma Ave

The year was 1876. The three sisters had the most delicious secret. Their youngest sister, Edith, was engaged to be married. The lucky man, Aubrey Harcourt, was handsome and very rich – heir to one of the finest estates in England, about which Alice's mother was particularly pleased. The sisters' time was exclusively devoted to chattering about the details of Edith's autumn wedding, Edith's dress, Edith's veil, Edith's shoes, who should be invited, and where Edith would go on her honeymoon. Sisters as close as these couldn't be happier.

To add to their joy, Prince Leopold and his royal party had arrived in Oxford for the weekend to celebrate the many social activities linked to Commemoration week. Alice glowed as she accompanied the Prince to the elegant Commemoration ball. There was so much joy, so much to celebrate, so much to look forward to.

Edith, Alice, Lorina

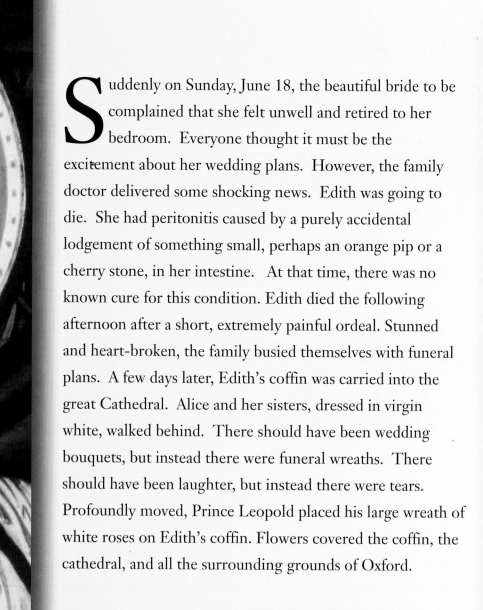

Suddenly on Sunday, June 18, the beautiful bride to be complained that she felt unwell and retired to her bedroom. Everyone thought it must be the excitement about her wedding plans. However, the family doctor delivered some shocking news. Edith was going to die. She had peritonitis caused by a purely accidental lodgement of something small, perhaps an orange pip or a cherry stone, in her intestine. At that time, there was no known cure for this condition. Edith died the following afternoon after a short, extremely painful ordeal. Stunned and heart-broken, the family busied themselves with funeral plans. A few days later, Edith's coffin was carried into the great Cathedral. Alice and her sisters, dressed in virgin white, walked behind. There should have been wedding bouquets, but instead there were funeral wreaths. There should have been laughter, but instead there were tears. Profoundly moved, Prince Leopold placed his large wreath of white roses on Edith's coffin. Flowers covered the coffin, the cathedral, and all the surrounding grounds of Oxford.

Alice turned to art to help her family heal. She commissioned Sir William Richmond to produce a moving portrait of Edith. A stained glass window was dedicated to Edith in Christ Church Cathedral.

It has been a pleasure to try to do you a little poem of your poor sister and in doing it I recollect one of the happiest periods of my life…I have made her looking towards the light…

Sir William Richmond in a letter to Alice Liddell

The Latin inscription on the window reads Ave Dulcissima Dilectissima Ave. "Hail our sweetest; our dearest Hail".

Ave Dulcissima Dilectissima Ave

"...what some of us have gone through , both in actual watching, and still more in terrible anxiety, cannot soon be overcome..."

Dean Liddell to his friend Robert Scott

"...you have no doubt heard of the great sorrow that has overtaken us - as sudden and unexpected as death by lightning..."

Dean Liddell to his friend Arthur Stanley

74

The pain of losing a beloved sister so suddenly, and in such a tragic way, was devastating. Alice never completely got over the death of Edith. Even as an old woman she would become emotional when people spoke about her beloved sister.

It was Regi Hargreaves who helped Alice at this difficult time in her life. He had fallen in love with her when he met her in 1875. He had patiently waited in the wings, after Prince Leopold, for the right moment to win her hand.

The year was 1880, three years after the death of Edith, when, in Regi's own words, his "long miniseries of uncertainty" came to an end. He proposed marriage and Alice accepted. She was 28 years old and ready to move forward with her life. Regi's patience and perseverance had paid off, for he had won not only Alice's hand, but more importantly, Alice's heart.

Alice's Wedding

" *My Dearest Regi,*

I did not say very much to you yesterday, I think, but can you guess a little bit how enchanted I was!

I hope it will be a real fairyland to us both as long as we are both permitted to enjoy it, dear;

'Wonderland' Come True to 'Alice' at Last."

—Alice Liddell to her husband

Each for the other and both for God

Inscription on Alice's wedding ring

"My darling Alice, I have been sitting and looking at your dear name and feeling as if I should like to go on writing it over and over again.....what can I write that is not summed up in those three little words, "I love you".

—Reginald Hargreaves to his wife

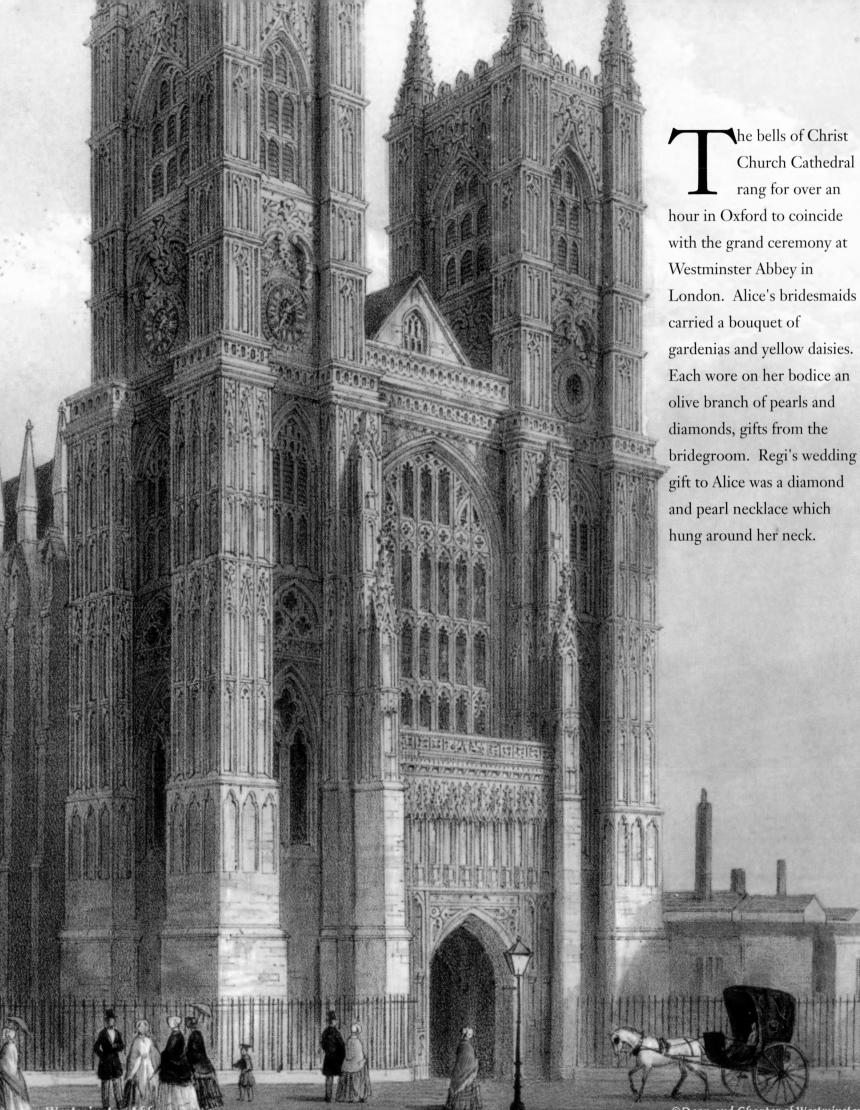

The bells of Christ Church Cathedral rang for over an hour in Oxford to coincide with the grand ceremony at Westminster Abbey in London. Alice's bridesmaids carried a bouquet of gardenias and yellow daisies. Each wore on her bodice an olive branch of pearls and diamonds, gifts from the bridegroom. Regi's wedding gift to Alice was a diamond and pearl necklace which hung around her neck.

Westminster Abbey

Alice, leaning on the arm of her father, looked like a fairy tale Princess. Her wedding dress was of rich spanish lace and white satin. On her head she wore a magnificent tulle veil with a circulet crown of diamonds.

The long line bodice is pleated into the waist at the back over the large bustle-bow and fastens with buttons at the front. The graduated lace collar rises from the throat to it's full height at the neck, the same lace, edged with satin ribbon, repeats around the shoulders, at the cuffs and at the base of the bodice. An "apron front" ruched drape of silk tulle over satin covers the front of the skirt, echoing the ruched satin sleeves. It is edged in a ruched band and finished with lace. The lower skirt is of a toning brocade, ending in flounces of lace over a pleated trim, all edged in blue ribbon.

The focus of the back of the skirt is a large blue satin bustle bow.

Alice's dress was re-created by artist Theresa Blake of Rossetti Couture.

I shall think of you tomorrow for you know how I have felt and sympathized with you…in your joys as in your sorrows.

Prince Leopold to Alice

Pinned to the front of Alice's dress was a beautiful horseshoe-shaped brooch. It was a wedding present from Prince Leopold, who did not attend. Perhaps he couldn't bear to see Alice married to another man.

Lady Hargreaves in her Lyndhurst Wonderland

For Alice, the 1880's were a Wonderland come true at last. Her new home, the Cuffnells estate in Lyndhurst, Surrey, was set on a hundred and sixty eight acres of beautiful Hampshire land. The main mansion, approached by two long sweeping driveways, stood on a separate private 17 acre park. There were vineries, ornamental lawns, and a large lake for boating and fishing expeditions. Regi had inherited a considerable fortune and was able to devote most of his time to leisure, sports, philanthropy, and his major passion: collecting trees for Cuffnells. An excellent cricketer, he had a cricket pitch laid at Cuffnells. The Cuffnells woods became famous among English arborists. Trees were imported from the tombs of the Chinese emperors of Mukden, the slopes of the Himalayas, and the Yosemite valley in California. Eucalyptus, Figs, Cypresses, Washington pines, Douglas firs, Redwoods, and Cedars were just a sampling of what could be found at Cuffnells. The rest of the estate consisted of a 150 acre agricultural farm.

A very large staff was required to run Cuffnells. The outdoor staff was comprised of a coachman, the groom, and numerous gardeners. This was separate from the large staff employed in the running of the Cuffnells farm.

Painting of Cuffnells Estate by local Lyndhurst artist Sir Charles Burrard

I remember going through the front door. There was a big hall with a beautiful staircase going up one side of it, and then you went through that to an ante room with a big table in the middle; and on that table, for anyone to look at and touch and pick up, was the original manuscript.

Mary Jean St. Clair –
Alice's granddaughter in a speech, June, 2009

The indoor staff included a lady's maid, a housekeeper, two cooks, the butler, a footman, a boot-boy, two kitchen maids, a scullery maid, three housemaids, and a laundry maid.

Building a strong marriage, as well as culturally and socially enriching her family's life, were Alice's major priorities. She was known to be a perfectionist when it came to the details in her new home. She devoted herself to enhancing Cuffnells' vast library with the finest poetry and literature. The walls of the elegant rooms in her grand home were adorned with beautiful artworks, many of them painted by Alice herself. Alice's Lyndhurst Wonderland became a focal point of country high society, and of course, Alice, its most famous society hostess. Important politicians, artists, and writers of the day, such as Rudyard Kipling and Arthur Conan Doyle visited Cuffnells to meet Alice, of Wonderland fame.

"First, there's the room you can see through the glass – that's just the same as our drawing room, only the things go the other way."
Alice – Through the Looking Glass

But her greatest happiness of all during these years were the births of three sons, Alan Knyveton Hargreaves, Leopold Reginald Hargreaves, and Caryl Liddell Hargreaves.

Luffnells
Lyndhurst
THE DRAWING ROOM

Upon the birth of her first child, Alan, Alice asked Lewis Carroll to be godfather. He declined. He really wished Alice had had a little girl. When asked if Caryl, Alice's 3rd son, was named after Lewis Carroll, Alice was ambiguous. She said she had named him after a literary character.

A lady in Alice's social position had many governesses and nannies, and didn't need to be involved in the day to day of raising children. Not Alice. She was very hands on when it came to raising her boys. She was interested in all their activities, including their academic and sporting successes, but perhaps even more importantly, the development of their characters. Naturally, as the years passed, reading about the adventures of Alice became the important bedtime evening event in the lives of Alice and her three boys, just as it was in every family in the English speaking world.

Alan was like his father: outgoing, charming, and a passionate sportsman. Everybody adored Alan, but most of all, Alice. Leopold (named after Prince Leopold) was academically more like Alice and also an enthusiastic sportsman. Although his family's nickname for him was Rex, Alice insisted the household staff call him "Master Leopold." Caryl was the most introverted of Alice's three boys. He became a gifted intellectual whose interests were mainly cultural pursuits.

THE NURSERY "ALICE"

*Alan
from his Mother
"Alice in Wonderland"*

Speak roughly to your little boy and beat him when he sneezes; he only does it to annoy, because he knows it teases…

**Lewis Carroll -
Alice's Adventures in
Wonderland**

Leopold, Caryl, and Alan Hargreaves

"Caryl is very well and read Alice in
Wonderland beautifully this morning."
Alice in a letter to her husband.

Even after his estrangement from Mrs. Liddell, Dodgson continued to keep in touch with Alice, and continued to present her with the new editions of his books and give her "Alice" memorabilia.

Shortly after Alice was married in 1880, her mother received a letter from Lewis Carroll asking for her new Lyndhurst address.

I want to send a copy of my new book to one, without whose infant patronage I might possibly never have written at all.

Lewis Carroll to Alice's Mother in 1883

Beyond the gifts of books and "Alice" memorabilia, there was also on occasion correspondence between them.

Dear Mrs Hargreaves,
Perhaps the shortest day in the year is not quite the most appropriate time for recalling the long dreamy summer afternoons of ancient times but anyhow if this book gives you half as much pleasure to receive as it does me to send, it will be a success indeed. Wishing you all happiness at this happy season. I am sincerely yours,
C. L. Dodgson

C. L. Dodgson to Alice Hargreaves
December 21, 1883

"My mental picture is as vivid as ever, of one who was through many years, my ideal child-friend. I have had scores of child-friends since your time but they have been a different thing . . ."

C. L. Dodgson to Alice Hargreaves
March, 1885

"I met Mr. Hargreaves (the husband of Alice) who was a stranger to me, though we had met, years ago, as pupil and lecturer. It was not easy to link in one's mind the new face with the olden memory – the stranger with the once so intimately known and loved Alice."

C.L. Dodgson in his diary 1888

Dear Mrs. Hargreaves,

I have a favour to ask of you, so please put yourself into a complaisant frame of mind before you read any further. A friend of mine, who is in the business involving ivory-carving, has had a lot of umbrella and parasol handles carved representing characters in *Alice* and *Through the Looking Glass*. I have just inspected a number of them: and, though nearly all are unsuited for use, by reason of having slender projections (hands, etc.) which would be quite sure to get chipped off, (thus spoiling to artistic effect), yet I found one (Tweedledum and Tweedledee) which might safely be used as a parasol-handle, without wearing out the life of the owner with constant anxiety. So I want to be allowed to present, to the original "Alice" a parasol with this as its handle — if she will graciously accept it, and will let me know what coloured silk she prefers, and whether she would like it to have a fringe. Wishing you and yours most sincrerely a very happy new year. I am most sincerely yours,
C.L. Dodgson

**– Charles Dodgson to
Alice Hargreaves, January 7, 1892**

*My grandmother Alice brought
up three sons and took part in
the local community except when
the other Alice intervened...then
she went to London for a
reception or a dinner...*

**Alice's grandaughter,
Mary Jean St. Clair, in a speech, 2009**

Alice was often seen riding and cycling around the village of Lyndhurst with her three boys. Her favorite pony was called Purton. She went everywhere with her beloved terrier dog called Quiz. Later in 1902, Regi bought her a new Silver Ghost Rolls Royce, registration R733. Her chauffeur, Mr. O'Dell, thoroughly enjoyed driving Lady Hargreaves.

All three of Alice's boys attended the famous English school, Eton. Leopold and Caryl went on to to study at Christ Church, Oxford. Alan went to Sandhurst to pursue a military career. Alice and her family lived in the beautiful village of Lyndhurst for over 50 years. Today the town still celebrates the Real Alice in Wonderland, not just because she was Carroll's inspiration, but because of the substantial contributions she made to the Lyndhurst community.

Scenes from "Alice in Lyndhurst" by Nick Mellersh

1908 Silver Ghost Rolls Royce courtesy of Beaulieu Abbey

Alice The Humanitarian

"One of the secrets of life is that all that is really worth doing is what we do for others."
Lewis Carroll

Entrance to the Cuffnells Estate

Alice shared this sentiment with Lewis Carroll. Charitable work was high on her list of priorities. She and her husband Regi became known for their dedication to community service. They were leaders in many of the important changes that happened in Lyndhurst over the next three decades, including the building of schools as well as entertainment facilities such as the local cricket club. While they were committed to prosperity, they were preservationists too. They stood against building a large railway station on Lyndhurst High Street which would have led to a tourist invasion of the village.

An impressive example of Alice's volunteerism was her extensive fundraising and community building activities for the Emery Down Women's Institute. The WI worked tirelessly to break down the social barriers between the rich and the poor in local communities. Once women over 30 were allowed to vote, the WI leadership focused on urging women to become more active citizens. The Women's Institute encouraged women to acquire new skills and to actively engage in issues that mattered to them and to their communities. On October 2, 1920, Alice was elected President of the WI. She continued as President until 1930, at which point she was made a life member.

The little Gold Key presented to Alice, President, Emery Down Women's Institute, 1920 - 1930.

The National Federation of Women's Institutes - First meeting in 1915 and today

Alice's family and volunteer work commitments in Lyndhurst made her visits to Christ Church less frequent. However, one particular charity project inspired her to volunteer her time. For years, Christ Church had operated a mission in the East End of London to support the building of new churches. Alice, a talented woodcarver, offered to create the vestry door for one of the churches.

"...she came upon a low curtain she had not noticed before, and behind it was a little door about fifteen inches high: she tried the little golden key in the lock, and to her great delight it fitted!"

Alice's Adventures in Wonderland

Alice's Door

The story goes that in World War II, the German airforce bombed the church and entire surrounding town to the ground. Soon afterwards, amidst the rubble, the church wardens discovered "Alice's door". It had miraculously survived and was completely intact. No doubt inspired by Alice, of Wonderland fame, the local community found a way to pick themselves up and start over again. Today Alice's beautiful door continues to inspire visitors who can see it at the north east end of the nave of another church, St.Frideswide Church in Osney, Oxford, where it was sent after the war.

St.Frideswide Church, Oxford

Perhaps the greatest contribution that Alice initiated with Carroll in her lifetime was their collaboration to help children in need with the proceeds from her book – the original manuscript given to her.

In 1883, Lewis Carroll wrote to Alice asking her permission to publish his original Christmas present to her, the handwritten manuscript – *Alice's Adventures Underground.* *Alice's Adventures In Wonderland* had now sold over 120,000 copies, and Carroll's publisher felt that the manuscript would have a big market too. Lewis and Alice also discussed having the profits from *Alice's Adventures Underground* donated to needy children.   Alice thought this was a very good idea, and fine tuned it a little, suggesting that the monies from their project be given to children's hospitals and convalescent homes for sick children.

The not-for profit book venture launched in 1886 and was hugely successful; in 1891 Dodgson invited Alice to tea to celebrate.

Over the next three decades, a number of projects for children and children's hospitals in the UK and the US were launched, using proceeds from the book and other monies from fundraisers linked to the book. Alice was patron of two of these initiatives, namely the Helpers of Wonderland League and the Lewis Carroll Memorial Fund. In addition, the St. Mary's Hospital Appeal in London was endorsed by Alice Liddell, and her photograph together with that of Lewis Carroll hung in the ward.

"Your adventures have had a marvellous success – have now sold over 100,000 copies and have sent hundreds to be read by sick children."
Charles Dodgson to Alice Liddell Hargreaves

I have been to say goodbye to one or two today and I found it very hard. I went to tea with Mr. Dodgson in the evening.
Alice in a letter to Regi December 9th, 1891

You would probably prefer to bring a companion; but I must leave the choice to you, only earmarking that if your husband is here, he would be most (deleted) very welcome.
Lewis Carroll to Alice Liddell Hargreaves

The telegraph boy came up the East Driveway to the Cuffnells house on May 9, 1915 to deliver an envelope that would shatter their lives. Captain Alan Hargreaves had been killed in action while heroically leading his men into battle near Fromelles, France.

There was more tragedy to follow. On September 25, 1916, after several months of brutal fighting, Rex was mortally wounded in combat.

"He was hit as we got to the German trench. He lay there all day and he was so patient and confident about himself that I had hopes that he might recover although we knew he was hit in the stomach...but he died the next day." **Rex's Commanding Officer to his parents**

Rex was posthumously awarded the Military Cross.

We must remember that children are only lent to us by God.

Alice in her diary after the death of her sons

Captain Alan Hargreaves

Captain Rex Hargreaves

"The Captain led us over the German trench....I am sorry to say the captain was one of the first hit."

Letter from Alan's commanding officer to Regi and Alice

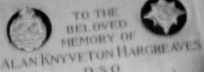

The double loss of their two beloved children within 17 months of one another left Regi and Alice grief stricken. They clung to the hope that their last remaining child, Caryl, would be returned home safely to them. Finally at the end of 1916, Caryl, was recalled to England.

Regi never recovered from the deaths of Alan and Rex. His spirit was forever broken. Silence and deep depression overcame him. Alice, while grieving herself, remained stoic for her beloved husband, supporting him through a long, slow decline in his health to his eventual death.

So we through this world's waning night
May, hand in hand pursue our way;
Shed round us order, love and light,
And shine unto the perfect day

Poem by Alice Liddell to
Regi, her husband

In a small blue envelope, he left this note for his beloved Alice in Wonderland:

"God bless you and keep you for all your love and care for me. No words of mine can express what you have been to me."

Reginald Hargreaves to his Alice, 1926

When midnight mists are creeping,
and all the land is sleeping.

Around me tread the mighty dead,
and slowly pass away…

Lyrics to the song
Dreamland **by Lewis Caroll**

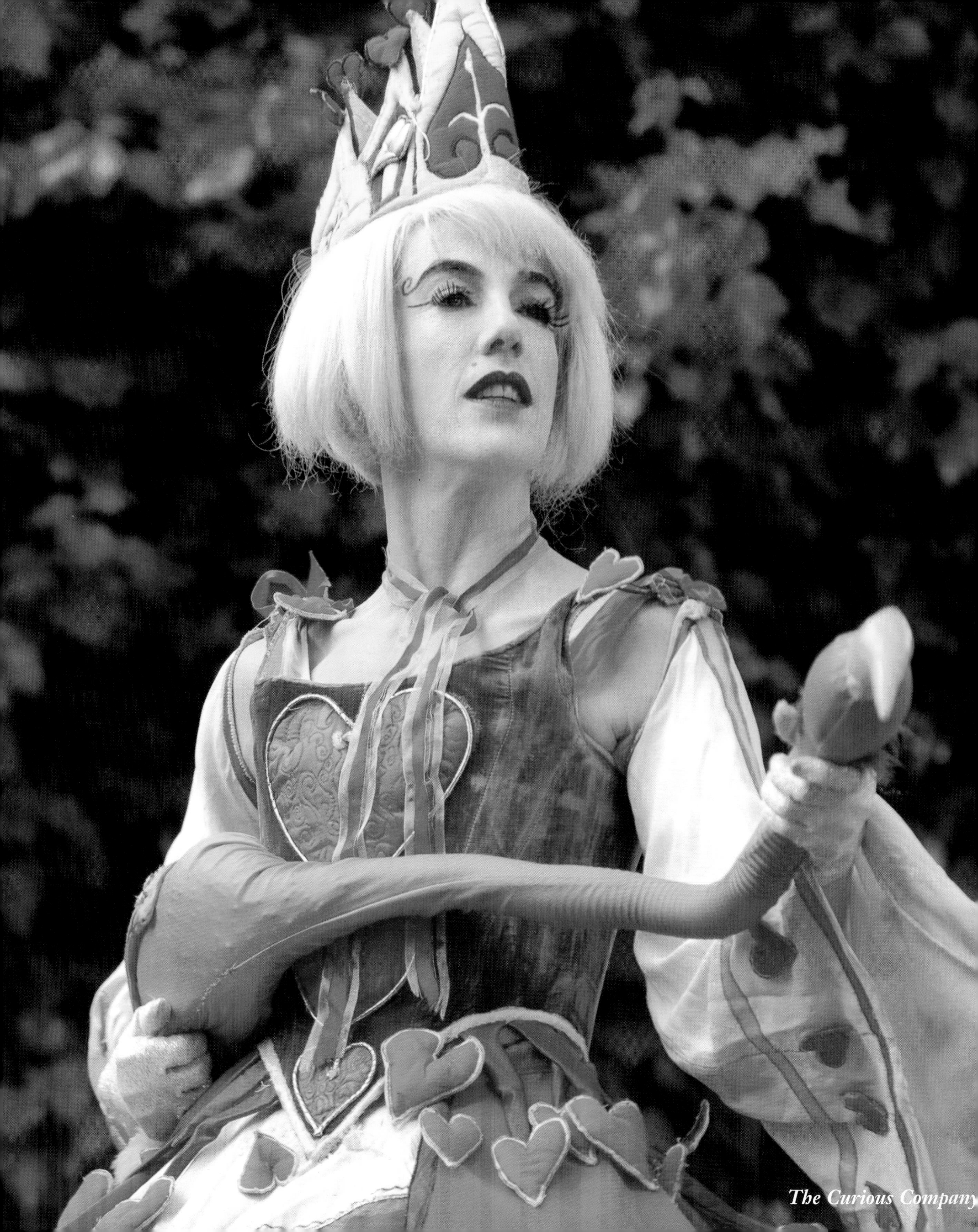
The Curious Company

"I thought of us, our world, as a self-satisfied Dodo bird. Doomed to eventual extinction but saved for a moment by the hope for new life in the egg. Every sculpture I make is a kind of self-portrait. This one is a little more dim-witted than most."

–Tom Otterness

Photo by Nicholas Walster

Sculpture by Tom Otterness

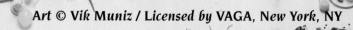
Art © Vik Muniz / Licensed by VAGA, New York, NY

Return To Wonderland

Alice and Dr. R

She desperately needed to raise money. Under the terms of his father's will, Regi was not allowed to leave Cuffnells to Alice. It had to pass to the eldest male heir, Caryl. Caryl let his mother stay there, but Alice was faced with huge maintenance costs and death duties (estate taxes) still owing. Additionally, Caryl had married and his wife was expecting a child. They needed money too. A sign was put up on the Cuffnells estate: "Rent This Historic Mansion." There were no takers. And then one morning, a group of American tourists rang the great Cuffnells doorbell asking if they might be permitted to see Alice's manuscript. As always, it was kept on a large table in the anteroom off the grand Cuffnells foyer. Alice considered it to be one of her most precious possessions, but she never looked at it for its financial value. Now she needed to. Alice sought the advice of Sotheby's.

"After love, book collecting is the most exhilarating sport of all."

Dr. R

His name was Dr. Abraham Simon Wolf Rosenbach (Dr. R to his friends). He was bright, successful, and flamboyant. The New Yorker called him the "Napoleon of Books," while the London tabloids preferred "the Terror of the Auction Room". He owned some of the finest book collections in the world, including the Folger Shakespeare Library and the Huntington Library. He had helped his private book clients, including J.P Morgan, Lessing Rosenwald, Eldridge Johnson, and Harry Elkins Widener build some of the greatest American research libraries in the world. Dr. R's mission in life was to acquire great books, ensure they got the care and preservation they needed to increase their value, and then, most importantly, make them accessible to the general public.

Rosenbach Museum & Library, Philadelphia

Sotheby's advised Alice that her manuscript was very valuable indeed. April 3, 1928 was the date set for the sale. As the big day drew near, the substantial press coverage put more pressure on Alice. Members of the British public feared that one of the most prized of all British literary possessions would finish up in the hands of an American. Protestors wrote to Alice, begging her to stop the auction and keep the British manuscript where it belonged - in England! She responded to some of the letters individually.

31 March 1928 Cuffnells Lyndhurst

Dear Mr Spooks,
Thank you very much for your letter. I am sorry about the M.S.S. (manuscript) of the Wonderland - Perhaps it may stay in England after all. All this stir has been made so late in the day that it did not seem possible to withdraw the little book from the auction. You write about the chance of calling here one day when motoring by. Pray come and call...
Yours truly
Alice Pleasance Hargreaves

Cuffnells Lyndhurst April 1928

Dearest Caryl,
There is such a lot to tell you about preliminaries to the Alice Sale...On the friday before the sale came an offer of 5000 and a promise to present the manuscript to Christ Church. I referred them to Sotheby's who refused them forthwith. I had a letter from the Director of the British Museum asking what price I could name. I answered at the last moment that I did not think I could withdraw the manuscript from Sotheby's hands. "another and another" letter from people - I referred them all to Sotheby's. On Monday I went to London and lunched with Ina. On returning to my club where I had left my luggage I found a message from Sotheby's asking me if I would call as there was an important point to discuss so greatly wondering I went over to Sotheby's. Mr Des Gras rather seriously put before me the offer that had just been made of 10,000. At one moment I very nearly took it, after finding out he would not object – he kept on saying "it may fetch more, on the other hand it may fetch less, – one can't say." – and in the end I said no, let it go on: – ...I am sending separately cuttings from the papers.
Please keep them.
Your loving Mother
APH

A Christmas Gift to a Dear Child in Memory of a Summer Day.

At 1 pm on April 3, 1928, three hundred spectators filled Sotheby's auction room in London.

"*I have seen men hazard their fortunes, go on long journeys halfway around the world, forge friendships, even lie, cheat and steal, all for the gain of a book.*"
ASW Rosenbach

"*Very young children eat their books, literally devouring their contents. This is one reason for the scarcity of first editions of Alice in Wonderland and other favorites of the nursery.*"
ASW Rosenbach

Rosenbach Museum & Library, Philadelphia

JOHN LESLIE fecit

Cuffnells, Lyndhurst 10th April 1928

Dearest Caryl,
I suppose you will have heard of the wonderful sale of
the Alice before this reaches you. It was a curious
moment or two when the bidding began and Mr Des
Gras said in a quiet voice £5000 - instantly capped by
£6000, £7000, and so on to £10,000 when there was a
wee halt - then on still to £15,400.....It is to be paid
over in about a month....I don't know what the per-
centage is, but at any rate what remains will pay my
death duties about which I was very anxious....I will
write again tomorrow. Your loving mother AP
Hargreaves"

Alice's letter to her son Caryl Hargreaves.

"The auction sale, which took place on April 3, 1928, was one of the most exciting ever held. I had been informed that the British Museum was interested in it and that they had instructed their representative to bid up to £12,000 at the sale. I thought that such a national treasure deserved a place in that great institution, and by agreement I refrained from bidding until the representative of the British Museum either won the manuscript or lost it. When however, their limit was exhausted, I entered the lists and finally purchased it for the sum of £15,400 or about $77,000. It was up to that time, a record in an English auction."

Dr. R. in a speech, May 1932.

What are the wild waves saying?
Alice where art thou now?

Though dear to us you've always
been, you're dearer to us now!

The Rosenbachs have been and
gone (just hear the dollars roar!).

And left some muddy footprints on
the British nursery floor.

The outcome of the Alice auction caused an Anglo-American uproar. Alice was pursued by the press as friends tried to hurriedly escort her to her awaiting car. She commented briefly before driving away: "It is a large sum of money and I do not yet know what I shall do with it." she said.

Immediately after the sale, Dr R. sent Alice a telegram. He also offered the Trustees of the British Museum the opportunity to buy back the manuscript for the cost price less $5000.

"A few hands clap. Then the crowd starts melting away. Over near the rostrum, an old woman, once little Alice, brushes a handkerchief across her eyes. Then she too vanishes.

Todays event has real significance for Anglo-American relations as much perhaps as the late lamented Geneva Convention.

CONGRATULATIONS. YOU DESERVE EVERY CENT YOU RECEIVED FOR IT! HOPE THE NATION WILL BE ABLE TO SECURE IT! BEST WISHES ROSENBACH

DR. A.S.W. ROSENBACH
(1876 - 1952)
Among America's most
influential rare book
dealers, he helped build
many of the nation's
great libraries. He and
his brother Philip
established the Rosen-
bach Museum & Library to
share their personal
collection with the pub-
lic. They lived on this
block from 1926 to 1952.
PENNSYLVANIA HISTORICAL AND MUSEUM COMMISSION 2008©

The British museum was unsuccessful in its efforts to raise the additional monies, and so Dr. R placed the literary jewel in his trunk with his other books and manuscripts and set sail for his beautiful home in Philadelphia. However, a moment of panic gripped Dr. R and the staff on the steamer. Shortly after they were out at sea, Dr. R's trunk mysteriously disappeared. After a thorough search and a sleepless night, the baggage clerk finally recovered it the next day. It was under the bed in the stateroom of a prominent banker. The precious manuscript did not remain in Dr. R's vault in Philadelphia for very long. Three weeks later, he sold it to his good friend and book collector, Eldridge R. Johnson (President of the Victor Talking Machine Company), for double the price, with the understanding that Johnson would arrange exhibitions in public libraries in several cities where everyone interested in *Alice's Adventures in Wonderland* would have an opportunity to see it.

As for Alice, the world media had got their first glimpse of the real thing and they were not going to let her go.

A Lifetime Achievement Celebration

In 1931, plans for a grand celebration to celebrate the birth of Lewis Carroll were underway in America. They were spearheaded by Columbia Professor Enrique Zannetti , Chairman of the Centenary Committee, and a number of American book collectors.

The Great Depression had struck and people in America desperately needed hope. They found it in Alice Pleasance Hargreaves.

Mrs Hargreaves, Original Of Fairy-Tale Heroine, Arrives Wide-Eyed But Undaunted By Tumult.

April 30, 1932
New York Times

"Today's 'Wonder-World' Needs Alice"
The New York Times Magazine 1932

"It gives me great pleasure to advise you in entire confidence that the trustees of Columbia University have voted to confer upon you the degree of doctor of letters in recognition of the place which your name occupies in English literature and of the remarkable contributions to that literature by Lewis Carroll to which your personality gave rise"

Columbia President Nicholas Murray Butler
letter to Alice Pleasance Hargreaves

"Dear Mr. Murray Butler,
I am looking forward with great pleasure to my visit to New York in May. I am extremely honoured by your intimation which I shall, of course, treat as confidential that you propose to confer a degree of honour on me."

Alice Pleasance Hargreaves
letter to President Nicholas Murray Butler

Courtesy of Columbia University

To the original Alice, England
When I was a little girl, I used to wonder what you were like and not until a few days ago, did I know you were real...

Fan letter to Alice Liddell from Tulsa, Oklahoma

"It is a great honor and a great pleasure to come over here and I think now my adventures overseas will be almost as interesting as my adventures underground were. I think that I have every prospect of having a most wonderful time as I had down the rabbit hole."

Excerpt from interview with Alice Pleasance Hargreaves -
Alice in U.S Land shown in movie theaters, 1932

Alice Lives, In Wonderland—And In Fact
New York Times Magazine, 1932

Real Alice Prefers The Cheshire Cat
New York Times, 1932

"Madam, I beg of you to forgive the boldness of a boy who was so thrilled to learn the address of The Alice who throughout his childhood was his much loved companion..."

**George Henry Singer,
Brooklyn, New York**

"When I was young I had to grow my neck long in order to get up to these heights. I think this is a much easier way."

Alice Pleasance Hargreaves commenting on the elevators at the Waldorf.

During her visit she stayed in a grand suite on the 39th floor of the Waldorf Astoria. Thousands of requests from American children begging her to autograph their Alice books had been sent. Alice agreed to make a national radio broadcast to the children of America. Her speech was broadcast to all of North America and Europe. Among the many *Alice Adventures in Wonderland* topics covered, she spoke about the monies from Lewis Carroll's books that were going to help children and children's hospitals in the US and the UK. Her speech was a huge success.

"Well, this IS grand!" said Alice. *"I never expected I should be a Queen so soon… Queens have to be dignified, you know!"*
–Through the Looking Glass

Curiouser and curiouser
–Alice's Adventures in Wonderland

On May 2, the degree ceremony took place at Columbia University. Alice was taken to the robing room where the gown and mortarboard were put on her. She looked very comfortable in the academic environment in which she had been raised. She was nearly overcome with emotion when she later commented, "It was a very lovely scene."

"Alice Pleasance Hargreaves, descendant of John of Gaunt, time-honored Lancaster daughter of that distinguished Oxford scholar whose fame will last until the english-speaking men cease to study the Greek language and its immortal literature; awaking with her girlhood's charm the ingenious fancy of a mathematician familiar with imaginary quantities, stirring him to reveal his complete understanding of the heart of a child as well as the mind of a man: to create imaginary figures and happenings in a language all his own, making odd phrases and facts to live on pages which will adorn the literature of the English tongue, time without end, and which are as charming as quizzical and as amusing as fascinating; thereby building a lasting bridge from the childhood of yesterday to the children of countless tomorrows — you as the moving cause of this truly noteworthy contribution to English literature, I gladly admit to the degree of doctor of letters in this university."

– Dr. Nicholas Murray Butler, President, Columbia University
Lewis Carroll Centenary, 1932

"I thank you, Mr. President, for the significant honor bestowed upon me. I shall remember it and prize it for the rest of my days, I love to think, however, unworthy I am that Mr. Dodgson – Lewis Carroll knows and rejoices with me."

– Alice Pleasance Hargreaves
speech – 1932

Alice and President Butler

"We honor today the little girl whose magic charm elicited from him seventy years ago the story that brought such delight to humanity."

—Professor Harry Morgan Ayres, Columbia University, 1932

The Low Rotunda Reading Room at Columbia University, May 2, 1932, where the Trustees of Columbia University conferred the degree of Doctor of Letters, honoris causa on Alice Pleasance Hargreaves.

Two days later on Alice's 80th birthday, May 4, 1932, the centenary celebrations continued in Columbia University's gymnasium. Over 2000 guests gave her a standing ovation as she walked with the aid of her cane to the microphone. Smiling shyly she began her speech; "I beg to thank you for your great kindness in inviting me to attend this celebration of the centenary of my childhood friend. He was the ideal friend of childhood…"

A magnificent decorative panel had been constructed to feature all the characters from *Alice's Adventures in Wonderland*. The Hunter College and Barnard College all women glee-clubs sang selections from the suite, "Alice in Wonderland," by Edgar Stillman, accompanied by the Columbia Orchestra.

"My drawing was inspired by John Tenniel, whose marvelous pen and ink creations for the book brought Alice to life in the same manner Alice Pleasance Hargreaves breathed life into the visualization of 'Alice' for Lewis Carroll. The ongoing fantasy of the 'real' Alice versus the 'fictionalized' Alice, captivated my own imagination, inspiring me to create a brand new Alice with linework inspired by Tenniel. This brings it all back full circle!"

Art and Inspiring words by Mark Steele

Alice cutting her cake at the Waldorf

"Famous literary heroines do not always come up to expectations, but Mrs. Reginald Hargreaves, who celebrated her eightieth birthday yesterday and made her little speech at Columbia, is all that Alice's millions of devoted admirers would wish her to be. Through the years she has kept the unassuming modesty and charm that made her Alice. And that now makes her a guest with whom the country is delighted..."

World Telegram, May 5, 1932

The Waldorf hotel hosted the 80th birthday party for Alice. The little girl with the clear blue eyes and the far-away look was now a beautiful woman of 80, and everyone seemed to have fallen in love with her. She was modest. She was elegant and she had a great sense of humor. There were luncheons and dinner parties with New York's royalty, including the Whitneys and the Roosevelts. Alice enjoyed touring the city, attending the Broadway productions of "Reunion in Vienna" and "Face the Music", and seeing the gangster movie "Scarface".

"Oh dear, we shall be late"

Alice and her son, Caryl Hargreaves, traveled to Philadelphia to meet with Dr. R, Eldridge Johnson, Arthur Houghton and Morris Parrish. Dr. R hosted a luncheon for Alice at his Delancey Place home which is just next door to the Rosenbach Museum today.

"We had a very good luncheon with plenty of good wine. After luncheon, a great photographing of APH. E. Johnson perfectly overcome with joy because APH suggested that he should be photographed with her," Caryl Hargreaves noted. "Eldridge Johnson towering over her, had the time of his life showing off the gadget-trimmed, watertight, fireproof, portable steel safe-deposit box which he had made to house the precious manuscript so that it would suffer no harm as it traveled on his yacht in the tropical seas," noted Edwin Wolf, Rosenbach's biographer.

Is it just coincidence? Or, did Alice cast her inspiring spell just one more time during the course of this wonderful luncheon at the home of Dr. R. On November 6, 1948, Dr. R and some of those present at this luncheon arranged to buy back Alice's manuscript. It was presented to the Archbishop of Canterbury in England, who accepted it on behalf of the British Museum from a group of American donors who wished to thank "the noble people who held Hitler at bay for a long period single-handedly" during World War II.

Dear Dr. Rosenbach,
The photographs duly arrived safe and sound, and I am very much obliged to you for sending them to me, and I think it is extremely kind of Mr. Eldridge Johnson to have autographed a copy for me. I shall take very great care of it. Pray remember your promise to let me know if, and when you pay another visit to England.
Yours sincerely,
Alice Pleasance Hargreaves
Rosenbach Museum & Library, Philadelphia

The Hollywood Alice

Not surprisingly, the global press coverage that followed Alice everywhere she went, helped to inspire Hollywood to make a movie based on *Alice's Adventures in Wonderland*. Disney first wanted to make an animated feature in the early 1930's. Paramount, however, beat Disney to it with a live film version they called *Alice in Wonderland*. In 1933, Paramount Pictures launched a search on both sides of the Atlantic to find the perfect actress to play Alice in their major motion picture.

"With that costume I was transformed in their minds to the person they had read about as children. My identity was gone. I no longer existed as Charlotte Henry."

Charlotte Henry on her role as Alice

Seven thousand eager young applicants on both sides of the Atlantic auditioned for the role of Alice. The most famous actresses of the day (including Mary Pickford) were turned down. It was publicized that "the real Alice" would approve the final choice. Finally, an unknown 19 year old named Charlotte Henry got the role. Gary Cooper (the White Knight), W.C. Fields (Humpty Dumpty), and Bing Crosby (Mock Turtle) made up the star studded cast of the costly production. A special screening to premiere the movie was arranged at the home of Alice Hargreaves.

Alice Moves to a New Wonderland

She was suddenly taken ill while out for a drive with her chauffeur in early November, 1934. She went into a coma. The world media followed her illness daily as if she were a queen. She died in her sleep on November 16th. The tributes and the flowers poured in. Everyone needed to celebrate her; to say goodbye…before she moved on to her new Wonderland.

THE GRAVE OF
MRS. REGINALD HARGREAVES
THE "ALICE" IN LEWIS CARROLLS
"ALICE IN WONDERLAND

From deep
down in
the underground,
the sun's bright rays,
her face
has found,
as all
her
subjects
gather round
to hear
her fairy tale.
Beyond the
roles that she has been,
beyond the nonsense
she has seen,
beyond it all,
the fairy queen
smiles
and
rules…
serene.

– C.M. Rubin

Sculpture by José de Creeft

Photograph Courtesy of Oxfordshire Museum Service.

The Real Alice in Wonderland for Sale

"In an exceptional sale such as this, we would naturally expect to see interest from our established client base – the loyal circle of serious collectors and dealers. The event attracted a far greater audience, beyond that regular group. I recall with the Alice Liddell auction that there were a great many interested parties. It seemed that a very substantial number of people wanted to own some little piece of her."
Philippe Garner, Auctioneer
"Lewis Carroll's Alice" Auction, 2001

This week Sotheby's is auctioning the world's greatest *Alice In Wonderland* collection – that owned by Alice herself.
Financial Times, June 2, 2001

Philippe Garner with Author C. M. Rubin

The Beggar Maid

"Alice vue par Lewis Carroll, la vente la plus excitante de l'année."

Michael Guerrin, Le Monde, June 1, 2001

Since the sale of Alice's manuscript in 1928, the Alice collector's market had been feverish. Individual photographs of Alice and her personal belongings had been sold by the family and fetched high prices from collectors around the world. On Wednesday, June 6, 2001, in an historic auction, Sotheby's sold off the bulk of Alice's personal belongings. The large collection, much of which had been in the library of Christ Church, Oxford, was put up for sale by Alice Liddell's granddaughter, Mary Jean St. Clair. It included Alice's letters, photographs, manuscripts, journals, and other family memorabilia. There were viewings around the world as well as glitzy PR events in Los Angeles (attended by Kathryn Beaumont, the voice of Disney's Alice), Chicago, and New York, prior to the main auction which took place at Sotheby's New Bond Street offices in London. Total sales were in the millions.

BRITISH RED CROSS SOCIETY

FOR WAR SERVICE 1914 - 1918

Photographs Courtesy of Oxfordshire Museum Service.

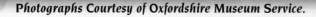

"Auktion Mit Alice"

Wirtschartswoche May 31, 2001

"Alice Liddell, the 'real Alice in Wonderland', is seen by many as more fascinating than the fiction she inspired."

Daily Telegraph, London, 2001

"Foto della vera Alice venduta a 600 millioni."

Corriere Della Sera - June 8, 2001

It is hardly surprising that the sale of the personal effects of Alice Liddell, the original Alice In Wonderland attracted such great interest...rarely have the dealings of the auction room played so touchingly on the heart strings.

Daily Telegraph, London June 7th, 2001

Jewel
Goodbye Alice in Wonderland

Jewel: Goodbye Alice in Wonderland
Courtesy of Rhino Entertainment Company

"Alice Liddell has a unique place in literature. She is the inspiration for the best-loved children's story in English literature."

Associated Press, 2001

134

Dear Alice,

Since we jumped into the rabbit hole in the Fall of 2006 to try to understand your life story, our journey has been filled with fantastic tales and Alice adventures in many different wonderlands around the world. We have combed the places where you grew up - London, Oxford, Lyndhurst and Llandudno - for stories of your life and legacy. We connected with Alice fans in Canada, Russia, Japan, Australia, Korea and from various parts of the United States, including Philadelphia, New Jersey, Texas, Ohio, California, Chicago and New York. We have read your personal correspondence to your family and friends at both the joyful and sad times of your life. We have poured over the hundreds of press articles and books written about you during and after your lifetime. We have been blessed with the guidance of passionate librarians and curious curators of the Alice story. And we began to understand the magnitude and beauty of your life.

Deciding how to tell our readers your story was another enormous challenge. We had our opinions of course, and wanted our individual voices to be heard, but we realized that so many others wanted to participate and that they often had facts and wisdom to share. We believe we found ways to be inclusive that were worthy of their knowledge.

We also wanted to tell your story in a way that would be up to your creative standards. You were an artist. Your water colors and sketches deeply moved us. Your talent as a wood carver inspired us. As artists, we felt the art in our story was as important as the words, as you so beautifully put it: "What good is a book without the pictures and conversations?" We reached out to artists, museums, and libraries around the world and they became inspired by our project too. So our book is not just filled with the photos from your family albums, but also with the photographs, illustrations, and sculptures of artists who were inspired by Alice's Adventures In Wonderland through the ages.

Who would have imagined that a book would take you on a fantastical journey that culminated in your becoming one of the most celebrated women of all time? When difficult circumstances forced you to give up this precious belonging, you understood the significance. We believe you went to America in 1932 with the desire to win it back for your country. Your unforgettable public appearances inspired the good people of America to ultimately return your book to England, where it rightfully belonged.

We would like to thank you for leaving a trail of precious breadcrumbs that enabled us to create this book about your life and legacy. We are inspired by your creativity and intelligence, your never failing courage, and by the example you set as wife, mother, and leader in your community during the most difficult of times. You handled your role as the exemplar of Alice's Adventures In Wonderland while establishing your own personal identity. We would love to think that wherever Lewis Carroll is, he agrees with our point of view. We would love to hope that wherever you are, you are pleased with your legacy, and rejoice in the knowledge that the real Alice is still thriving!

Very curiously yours,

C.M. Rubin and Gabriella Rose Rubin

The Producers of this book wish to thank Nancy Rosin
for her guidance and assistance on Victorian art.
Nancy Rosin is the owner of Nancy Rosin's Victorian Treasury

Select Bibliography of references cited in
The Real Alice in Wonderland

"Alice in Lyndhurst". *Play and Pantomine Scripts.* Nov. 2009. http://www.nick.mellersh.net

Bodner, George. *The Lion and the Unicorn, ASW Rosenbach Dealer and Collector.* John Hopkins University Press, 1998.

Carroll, Lewis and Oxenbury, Helen (art). *Alice's Adventures in Wonderland.* Walker Books Ltd, 1999.

Carroll, Lewis. *Through the Looking Glass.* Dover Publications Inc., 1999.

Carroll, Lewis. *Alice's Adventures in Wonderland* and *Through the Looking Glass.* The Modern Library, 2002.

Clark, Anne. *The Real Alice:* Michael Joseph Ltd., 1981.

Clark, Anne. *Lewis Carroll A Biography.* J.M. Dent & Sons, 1979.

Clark, Anne with additions by Angela Trend. *Wonderland come true to Alice in Lyndhurst. The Alice Adventure.* Lyndhurst, 2009.

Cohen, Morton N. ed. *The Letters of Lewis Carroll, Vol 1 and 2.* Macmillan, 1979.

Cohen, Morton N. *Lewis Carroll: Interviews and Recollections.* Macmillan, 1989.

Collingwood, Stuart Dodgson. *The Life and Letters of Lewis Carroll.* Thomas Nelson & Sons, 1899.

Eriksson, Karin and Bjork, Christina. *The Other Alice.* Raben & Syogren, 1993.

Gardner, Martin. *The Annotated Alice.* Bramhall House, 1964.

Gordon, Colin. *Beyond the Looking Glass – Reflections of Alice and Her Family.* Harcourt Brace Jovanovitch, 1982.

Hargreaves, Caryl with Hargreaves, Alice. *"Alice's Recollections of Carrollian Days as told to Caryl Hargreaves by his Mother Alice".* The Cornhill Magazine, July 1932.

Leach, Karoline. *In the Shadow of the Dreamchild.* Peter Owen Publishers, March 1999.

Mrs. Hargreaves Remembers. By Lewis Carroll, Martin Wesley-Smith and Peter Wesley-Smith. Alliance Francaise Society, Sydney, Australia. July 1, 1997. Performance.

Neave, Nick and Douglas, Colin. *Like Carrying Coals to Newcastle:* Summerhill Books Newcastle Upon Tyne, 2009. Adamson, Noel. Newman Francis G., *Pontop Pike To The Tyne'* DVD insert in *Like Carrying Coals To Newcastle.* Summerhill Books Newcastle Upon Tyne, 2009

Prose, Francine. *The Lives of the Muses.* Harper Perennial, 2003.

Ruskin, John. *The Art of England. Lectures given in Oxford.* Lowe Press, 2008.

St. Clair, Mary Jean. *The Alice Adventure.* Interview. You Tube. January, 2010.

Stoffel, Stephanie Lovett. *The Life and Times of Alice and her Creator.* Abrams, Harry N. Inc. 1997.

Waggoner, Diane. *The Advent of Alice.* The Rosenbach Museum & Library, 1999.

Acknowledgements

The Authors are grateful to the following artists for permission to reproduce their work.

Annie Leibovitz

Bruce Fuller

David Cooper

Edwin Russell

Frances Broomfield

Helen Oxenbury

Ian Hemery

Jeanne Argent

John Paul Bland

Lizzy Rockwell

Louise Rennie

Madame Alexander Dolls

Mark Steele

Tatiana Ianovskaia

Theresa Blake

Tom Otterness

Vik Muniz

Virginia Ross

The Authors are grateful to the following organizations and people for permission to reproduce their images.

Alice's Shop, Oxford (Luke Gander)

Alice's Tea Cup, New York City (Haley Wynn)

Angela and Paul Trend

Beaulieu Abbey National Motor Museum (Jonathon Day and Margaret Rowles)

Columbia University (Jocelyn Wilk, Yaakov Sullivan and Paul Hond)

Guildford Borough Council (Diana Roberts and Su Kelland)

Imperial College Healthcare NHS Trust (Kevin Brown and Saffron Pinegar)

Llandudno Historical Society

LLyfrgell Llandudno Library (Mel Evans and Staff). Alice of Llandudno is dedicated to the memory of Geraint Wynne Morgan.

Museum of Natural History Oxford (Wendy Shephard)

Nancy Rosin's Victorian Treasury (Nancy Rosin)

National Federation of Women's Institute